49 Excuses for Getting the Most Out of Christmas

Copyright © 2018, 2022 by James Warwood

Published by Curious Squirrel Press

All rights reserved

No part of this book may be used, stored or reproduced in any manner whatsoever without written permission from the author or publisher.

Book cover design by: James Warwood
Book interior design by: Mala Letra / Lic. Sara F. Salomon

ISBN: 9781915646255
ebook ISBN: B07H4LQXV7

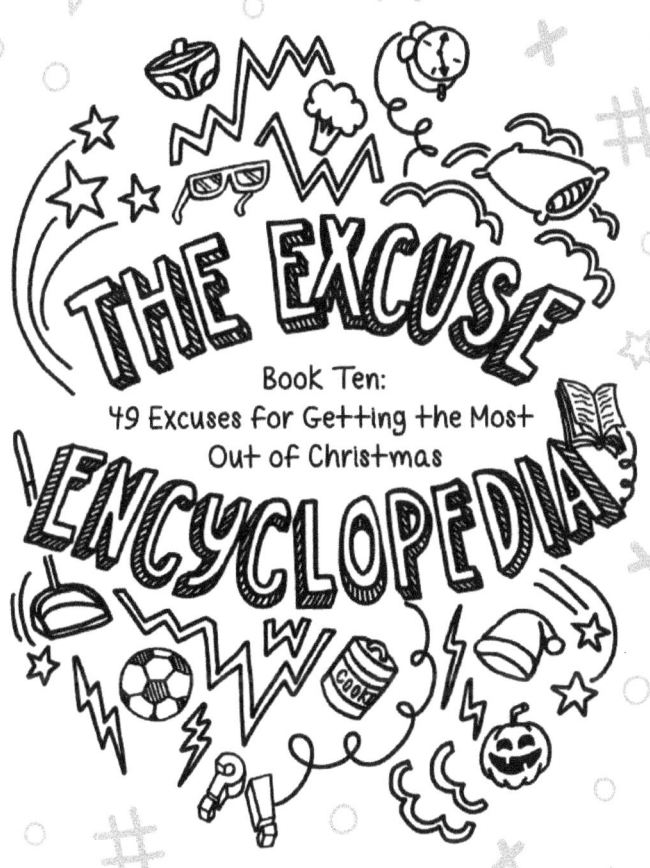

THE EXCUSE ENCYCLOPEDIA

Book Ten:
49 Excuses for Getting the Most
Out of Christmas

James Warwood

BOOK TEN

Excuses for Dodging the Dreaded Christmas Day Walk

CHRISTMAS EXCUSES

1. THE INDOOR WALK EXCUSE

Christmas dinner was delicious. Thank you, but you'll have to go on without me . . .

. . . I'm now so round I've lost the use of my legs. You all go on the Christmas walk and I'll stay at home and burn off the Christmas Dinner calories by rolling around the living room to 'Rockin' Around the Christmas Tree'.

2. THE SECURITY EXCUSE

Go on a walk? Now? Fine, but someone has to stand guard . . .

. . . All these lovely presents need to be protected against the Grinch, common thieves, master criminals, the Borrowers, and let's not forget Kevin. You know, the spotty kid next door who has sticky fingers and collects shiny things.

3. THE REPLACEMENT ANGEL EXCUSE

Oh no! Where did the angel on top of the Christmas Tree go? . . .

. . . It's a holiday disaster. Christmas is ruined. Unless, I don't go on the Christmas walk, dress like an angel, and perch on top of the tree with my trademark angelic smile.

4. THE GHOST EXCUSE

I can't go on the walk because I'm expecting an important visitor . . .

. . . Who? The ghost of Christmas Future. Apparently being a Scrooge, saying 'bah humbug', and not getting into the Christmas spirit will get you haunted. So if you want a better present next year you should leave me behind so that I can become a better person.

5. THE EMERGENCY CALL EXCUSE

Bad news. Just got off the phone with the Temp Agency...

... Father Christmas needs emergency workers to finish all his deliveries. They're offering double pay for working Christmas Day. It was an offer too good to refuse. My delivery rounds are Hungary, then Switzerland and finishing with Norway. Save me a mince pie.

Excuses for Forgetting Someone's Christmas Present

CHRISTMAS EXCUSES

6. THE ME EXCUSE

Ah. Your Christmas present . . . Your present is . . . erm . . .

. . . Me! I know, best Christmas present EVER. Here are some important instructions to keep your new present healthy and happy. Bedtime is 23:00, it needs a chocolate coin every hour, and if it eats a vegetable it'll turn into a little monster.

7. THE POSTMAN EXCUSE

Where's your present? I sent it in the post...

... Come to think of it the parcel should have arrived by now. If your postman is wearing stripy gloves with a matching scarf and bobble hat then make sure you report them for postal theft.

8. THE ENLIGHTENMENT EXCUSE

Sit down, cross your legs and close your eyes . . .

. . . Meditate like this for three years and you'll gain the best present this life can possibly offer – inner peace. You can thank me in three years' time. Now then, if you need me, I'll be seeking inner awesomeness by completing my new video game I got for Christmas.

9. THE PERFECTION EXCUSE

You know how I'm the perfect child?

. . .

. . . Well, my Christmas present to you is one whole week of intensive training. I'll teach you how to be perfect just like me.

10. THE SPIRIT PET EXCUSE

I found the perfect present for you . . .

. . . I discovered your spirit animal. It's this toad. So, my Christmas present to you is your soul pet. He lives at the bottom of the garden, enjoys long walks on the beach and answers to Kevin.

Excuses for Leaving your Brussels Sprouts

CHRISTMAS EXCUSES

11. THE DOGS DINNER EXCUSE

Why have I left my Brussels sprouts?
. . .

. . . Because these Brussels sprouts are my Christmas present to the dog. I can't wait to give them to him. He's gonna love 'em!

12. THE BELGIAN HERITAGE EXCUSE

Did you know that I'm half Belgian . . .

. . . In my homeland we never eat Brussels sprouts on Christmas Day. Never. It is considered an offence to eat anything green at all. We only eat Belgian chocolate.

13. THE REINDEER SNACKS EXCUSE

You know how we leave carrots out on Christmas Eve for the reindeer . . .

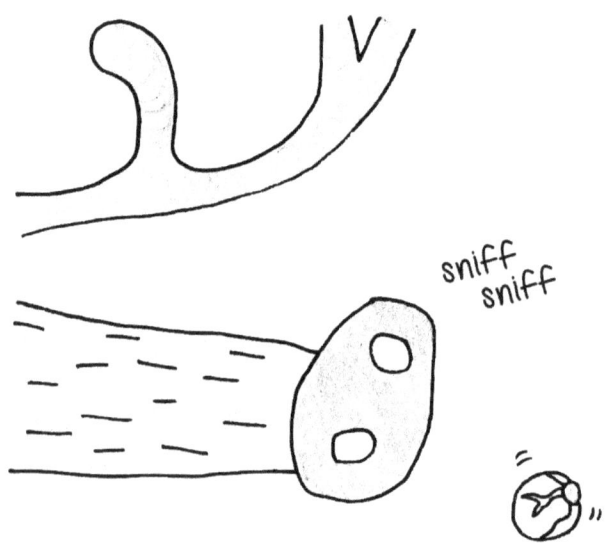

. . . Well, someone told me that we also have to leave Brussels sprouts outside for the return journey. Apparently, the extra gas helps the reindeer get home to the north pole in time for supper.

14. THE VEGAN BAUBLES EXCUSE

I have had a wonderful business idea...

...Vegan-Friendly Baubles. They're Brussels sprouts, which means they're both Christmassy and edible (but definitely not suitable for children).

15. THE BANNED EXCUSE

The Queen of England has banned Brussels sprouts! . . .

. . . She announced it in her Christmas Speech while you were on the loo. I'm afraid that it would be an act of high treason against the royal crown of the British Monarchy to eat them now.

Excuses for Getting Up Early on the Big Day

CHRISTMAS EXCUSES

16. THE ALARM EXCUSE

Who set the alarm clock for 5am?!?

. . .

. . . Well it wasn't me, so it must have been Rudolf. You know, the red-nosed reindeer. He's such a prankster. So, now that everyone is up and wide awake, which presents are for me?

17. THE CLOCKS EXCUSE

Look, it's 7am!! . . .

. . . If you don't believe me then go ahead and check every single clock in the house. Admittedly the oven clock was the hardest to change but definitely worth it.

18. THE BREAKFAST EXCUSE

I couldn't sleep because I was really, really hungry . . .

. . . So, I decided to make a Christmas breakfast for everyone. I didn't know what you'd like to eat so I made quite a lot. Eat up before it gets cold.

19. THE NIGHTMARE EXCUSE

I can't sleep. I had a terrible nightmare...

... I dreamt that I'm going to sleep in past 7am. Gulp! Then I wake up shivering in a pool of cold sweat terrified that I'm going to sleep in on Christmas Day.

THE HORROR!!!

20. THE WEATHER UPDATE EXCUSE

Good morning and welcome to your personal early morning weather update...

THURS	FRI	SAT	SUN
🌧️	⛈️	💨	☀️

...You can expect a wonderful start to the day, full of smiles and laughter and light showers of wrapping paper. Over lunchtime the temperature is set to shoot up (for the turkey) followed by naps on the sofa. When we reach the evening a cloud of competitiveness will descend with potential for outbreaks of thunder and lightning (depending on who wins the family board game).

Excuses for Having Chocolate for Breakfast

21. THE CHOCOLATE ON TOAST EXCUSE

I normally have chocolate spread on toast for breakfast . . .

. . . But, seeing as it is Christmas Day, I've decided to skip the spread and just have chocolate on toast. How long do you think I should put it in the microwave for so that it goes lovely and melty?

22. THE REPLACEMENT CUTLERY EXCUSE

For breakfast I'm going to have a simple bowl of cereal . . .

. . . in a bowl made of chocolate. And I'll eat it with a spoon made of chocolate. Oh, and I'll use chocolate milk and drink the dregs at the bottom of the bowl with a chocolate straw.

23. THE HEATWAVE EXCUSE

There's going to be a Christmas heatwave. Quickly, eat all the chocolate before it melts . . .

. . . Oh, hang on. I was looking at the weather forecast for Australia by accident. Whoops.

24. THE HOT CHOCOLATE EXCUSE

Good morning and Happy Christmas. I've made you a lovely big mug of hot chocolate . . .

. . . What would I like for breakfast? I'd like a lovely big mug of cold chocolate please.

25. THE FOUNTAIN EXCUSE

Ta-da. Here is your wonderful Christmas present...

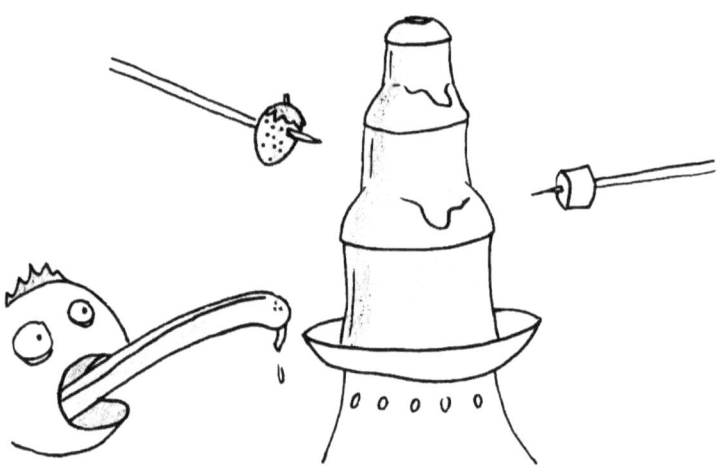

... The Choco-Fountain 5000. I thought you'd want to give this baby a go straight away so I set it up ready for Christmas morning breakfast.

Ways to Capture Father Christmas

CHRISTMAS EXCUSES

26. THE SLEEPING POWDER EXCUSE

I made bedtime drinks . . .

. . . The coffee is for me and the milk is for Father Christmas. Did I slip sleeping powder into his milk so he'd fall asleep and leaving his magical sleigh full of presents unguarded? That's a terrible accusation to make. Now if you'll excuse me, I have a long night ahead.

27. THE SURPRISE ATTACK EXCUSE

So, here's the plan . . .

. . . Once Father Christmas falls down the chimney, I'll cover him in shaving cream and you'll quickly shave his beard off. Then we'll post his picture on the internet and wait for his mum to identify him and tell him off for being out so late.

28. THE TRAP EXCUSE

How do you catch an old man who's been on his feet all day and all night? . . .

. . . Easy. Leave a pair of slippers next to a comfy chair with an episode of Countdown on the TV. It's almost too easy!

29. THE PLANE TICKET EXCUSE

Right then, I'm off . . .

. . . My plane to Australia awaits. But don't worry, I won't miss Christmas. I'll spend Christmas Day in the down-under and quickly take a return plane home. That way I'll have two attempts to snap a photo of Father Christmas.

30. THE STRAY ELF EXCUSE

Shh. I'm not Matt, I'm Kevin the lost workshop Elf . . .

. . . My plan is to hitch a lift with Father Christmas to his secret lair in Lapland. Then I'll sneak into his bedroom, find his passport, and bring it back to prove he really does exist and reveal his real name to the world.

Excuses for Not Doing the
Christmas Washing Up

CHRISTMAS
EXCUSES

31. THE LEFTOVERS EXCUSE

Don't clear away the plates just yet . . .

. . . Christmas Dinner isn't finished. There is so much food left over I made it into a mountain. It may take all week to eat but we can't let anything go to waste.

32. THE NEW TECHNIQUE EXCUSE

Let's test my new washing up technique . . .

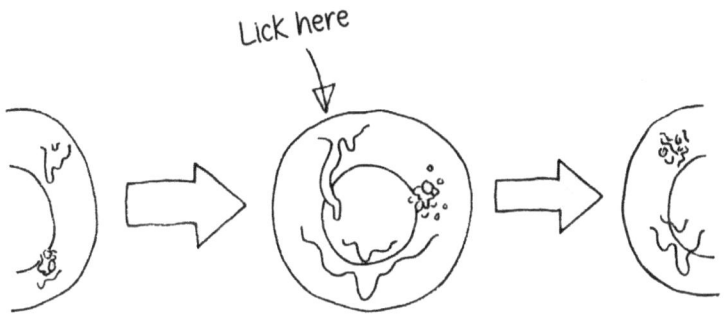

. . . Simply pass your empty plate to the left, lick it, then pass it on to the right. If my calculations are correct then I estimate that once the plates have gone around the table three to four times they will be spotless.

33. THE CAROL INSTRUCTIONAL EXCUSE

I've decided to re-enact my favourite Christmas Carols...

...So, I've asked granddad to have a nap for God Rest Ye Merry Gentlemen, the cat is wearing a grey pillowcase for Little Donkey, grandma is listening out for bikes and text notifications for I Heard the Bells on Christmas Day and I'm attempting to balance this delicious American snack on this tower of washing up for Ding Dong Merrily on High.

34. THE UNCLE CHRISTMAS EXCUSE

Last night we left cookies, milk and carrots for Father Christmas and his reindeer...

... Well, on Christmas Day night we have to leave our dirty dishes. Who for? For Uncle Christmas, of course (he was getting jealous of his older brother getting all the limelight).

35. THE TOAST EXCUSE

Before we do the washing up I'd like to give a toast . . .

. . . So, put your orders in. You can have peanut butter, chocolate spread or both.

Excuses for Not Taking Down
the Christmas Tree

36. THE NEW SONG EXCUSE

Good news. I've been commissioned by Christmas to write a new Christmas song . . .

. . . I call it 365 Days of Christmas. It's like 12 Days of Christmas but you can sing it every day of the year and celebrate Christmas all year round!

37. THE ALL-YEAR EXCUSE

Don't put the tree down!!! . . .

. . . I've made tree decorations for the rest of the year. Here's the New Year Decorations and we've got Pancake Day, Easter, Summer Holidays, and Hallowe'en decorations to look forward to.

38. THE BOXING DAY LUNCH EXCUSE

Time to take down the tree . . .

. . . Brian the beaver is working on it now. It will probably take him all week to finish his lunch, after all, he is only a little critter.

39. THE PHOTO TREE EXCUSE

No need to take down the Christmas Tree as I've transformed it in to a Picture Tree . . .

. . . No more edible baubles or silly tinsel in sight. Instead you can hang photos from the branches and my delightful art work.

40. THE BIRDS NEST EXCUSE

I was taking down the Christmas tree when I found a nest ...

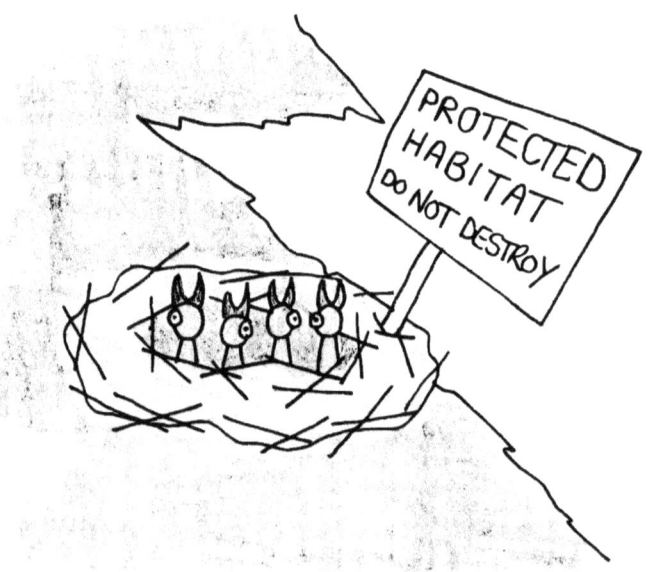

... A bird's nest. Look. Four little chicks nesting in our Christmas tree. Except this is no longer our Christmas tree, because it has now become their home. And we can't destroy their home, it's Christmas.

Excuses for Not Going to the Christmas Church Service

41. THE WRONG DATE EXCUSE

I want to go to Church on Jesus' real birthday...

... According to theologians we've all got it wrong. His birthday is 11th September and not 25th December. So, I'll be going to Church on 11th September to celebrate the birth of Jesus, I do hope there will be cake.

42. THE DAY OFF EXCUSE

Did you miss the memo? Jesus has given everyone the day off . . .

. . . Humanity has been told to stay at home in their pyjamas and watch Christmas movies all day. He really is a nice guy.

43. THE SNOWED IN EXCUSE

Look outside. It's snowing! . . .

. . . We shouldn't go to church in a blizzard. It would be a very dangerous journey. We should ask ourselves, what would Jesus do? Personally, I think he'd go sledging.

44. THE FANCY DRESS EXCUSE

Is the Christmas Day Church service fancy dress? . . .

. . . If not then it should be. Can I go as Baby Jesus?

45. THE INVITATION EXCUSE

Sorry, I can't go to church today . . .

. . . I found this at the bottom of my stocking. It's from Father Christmas. He has invited me to his church's Christmas Day service in Lapland. I'd better get going or I'll miss the first carol.

Excuses for Staying Up Really, Really Late

CHRISTMAS EXCUSES

46. THE LATE NIGHT SPEECH EXCUSE

We've all watched the Queen's Christmas Speech, it was a good one this year . . .

. . . This year she will also be doing a Late-Night Christmas Speech after the Royal Family's Christmas Bash. I hear it's wild, she'll probably be wearing a paper hat and slurring her words. Can I stay up to watch it?

47. THE BOARD GAMES EXCUSE

Let's play a board game before bed . . .

. . . Can Grandpa play? He always takes ages to take his turn. Which one takes longer? Scrabble, Monopoly or Trivial Pursuit?

48. THE ANOTHER ONE EXCUSE

Go on, have another glass of mulled wine . . .

. . . And then have another Baileys followed by a cheeky sherry. When you've fallen asleep in front of the telly I promise I'll go to bed on time and sleep like an angel.

49. THE PLEASE EXCUSE

But, but, but . . .

Mum... could I have a Cookie .... please?!

. . . It's the most special day of the whole year! . . . I want the opportunity to enjoy as much of Christmas Day as possible which means staying up until 23.59pm. To the very last minute. If I go to bed now I'll have to wait another 365 days. Please let me stay up late tonight.

BONUS: BIG PRESENT EXCUSE

So, I know that I've been a disappointment this year . . .

. . . but when Christmas Day arrives and I present you with this present you'll be glad that you put up with all my excuses.

BONUS: SURGERY EXCUSE

Sorry I'm late, Miss . . .

. . . I've been scheduled for emergency surgery to remove the Christmas Music that is stuck in my head. It's a risky procedure and it'll take four weeks to recover but I think you'll agree it'll all be worth it.

BONUS: CHRISTMAS EVE X 35 EXCUSE

Happy Christmas eve, eve, eve, eve, eve, eve, eve, eve, eve, eve, eve, eve, eve, eve, eve, eve, eve, eve, eve, eve, eve, eve, eve, eve, eve, eve, eve, eve, eve, eve, eve, eve, eve, eve, eve . . .

. . . What? No, there isn't thirty-five girls called Eve standing behind you. I just thought you might want to start celebrating Christmas early this year? I am available for mince pie and advent calendar tasting if needed.

BONUS: MARIAH CAREY EXCUSE

I had to go tell the singer, Mariah Carey something . . .

. . . I had to go all the way to Hollywood to tell that weirdo she can't have me for Christmas. I'm just a kid, that would be illegal and far beyond Father Christmas' abilities. I'm pretty sure he is not involved in human trafficking. I suggest you should go to Hollywood and do the same.

BONUS: LAST MINUTE PRESENT EXCUSE

This year I struggled to find you a Christmas present . . .

. . . but then last night I listened to a famous Christmas song and found some inspiration. You've got a pear tree in your garden, haven't you?

BONUS: MISTLETOE POISON EXCUSE

I really want to come to school today...

... but I've picked up a really bad case of mistletoe poisoning. Believe me, you don't want me spreading this around the school. No one will have any of their toes left.

BONUS: BAD BREATH EXCUSE

I've got horrific morning breath . . .

. . . I need a chocolate pallet cleanser as a Christmas breakfast. But what should I choose? Chocolate coin, chocolate log, advent calendar chocolate or the biggest chocolate from the Christmas tree?

BONUS: NO TIME EXCUSE

Sorry, there's no time to do the Christmas washing up . . .

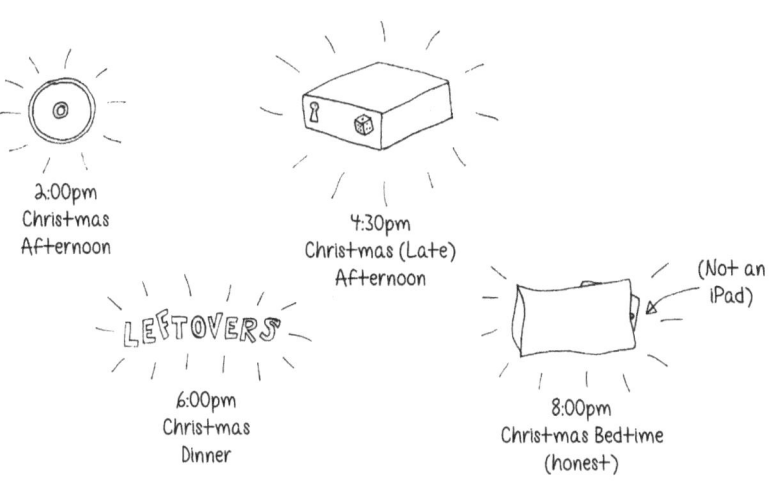

. . . I've got a very busy schedule. We'll just have to do the washing up next year.

BONUS: EXTENDED EDITION EXCUSE

Before we go to bed, let's watch one more Christmas film . . .

. . . How about the Home Alone Trilogy Extended Edition with an extra five hours worth of deleted scenes. Someone better go and make everyone some coffee as we're in for a looooooong night.

BONUS: YELLOW PAGES EXCUSE

To catch Father Christmas I've made a number of Yellow Page Ads...

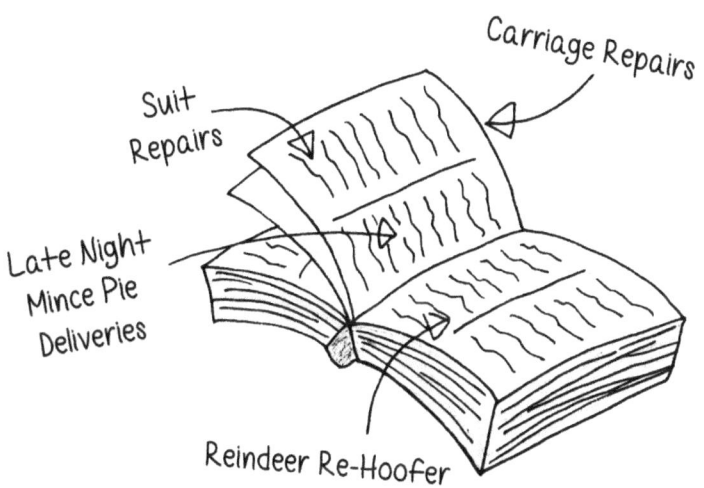

- Carriage Repairs
- Suit Repairs
- Late Night Mince Pie Deliveries
- Reindeer Re-Hoofer

... I'm hoping to get a call from the jolly red-suited man. If he needs a pit stop later tonight, and I'll be ready.

BONUS: CHRISTMAS EXAM EXCUSE

Wake up, wake up . . .

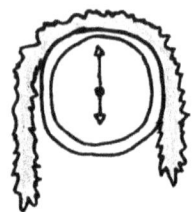

. . . the Christmas Exam is about to begin. It's a forty-five minute written exam followed by an all-day practical. You will receive your results on Boxing Day. If you pass I'll give you a hug every day for a whole year. If you fail I'll make it my mission to make sure you never touch the TV Remote for a whole year! Good luck.

BONUS: CHRISTMAS STRESS EXCUSE

I am the GREATEST GIFT GIVER of all time . . .

. . . and in order for me to work my magic I need the four weeks before Christmas off school. And if you grant me this leave of absence, I'll make sure your gift is the best one.

BONUS: HANUKKAH EXCUSE

Christmas only lasts one day . . .

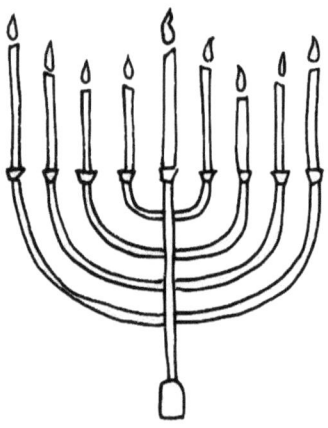

. . . However, I have just discovered that Hanukkah lasts for eight days. So, I'm now Jewish and need eight times as many presents than last year.

James Warwood is a writer and illustrator who lives on the borders of North Wales with his wife, two sons, and cactus (called Steve the Cactus).

He has a degree in Theology, which at the time seemed like a great idea, until he released he didn't want to become an RE Teacher. Instead, he writes laugh-out-loud middle grade fiction and non-fiction. He also fills them with his silly cartoons. He is the bestselling author of the EXCUSE ENCYCLOPEDIA and the TRUTH OR POOP SERIES.

James likes whiskey, squirrels, reading silly books, playing his bass guitar, and Greggs Sausage Rolls. He does not like losing at board games or having to writing about himself in the third person.

WHERE TO FIND JAMES ONLINE

Website: www.cjwarwood.com
Goodreads: James Warwood
Instagram: CJWarwood
Facebook: James Warwood

Want to join the
BOOKS & BISCUITS
CLUB?

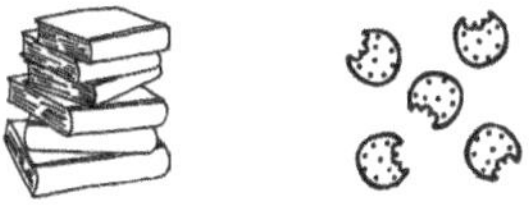

Scan me to sign up
to the newsletter.

MIDDLE-GRADE STAND-ALONE FICTION

The Chef Who Cooked Up a Catastrophe
The Boy Who Stole One Million Socks
The Girl Who Vanquished the Dragon

TRUTH OR POOP SERIES

*True or false quiz books.
Learn something new and laugh as you do it!*

THE EXCUSE ENCYCLOPEDIA

11 more books to read!

GET THEM ALL IN THIS 12 IN 1 BUMPER EDITION!

820-page compendium of knowledge with 180 BONUS excuses

Scan me to activate your

25% DISCOUNT

www.ingramcontent.com/pod-product-compliance
Lightning Source LLC
Chambersburg PA
CBHW041313110526
44591CB00022B/2903